THE
OTHER SIDE OF

Yes

SURRENDERING TO THE PURPOSES OF GOD

REV. DELPHINE REED

First published by AuthorHouse 05/04/04

ISBN: 1-4184-6529-1 (e-book)
ISBN: 1-4184-4084-1 (Paperback)

Library of Congress Control Number: 2004092130

This book is printed on acid free paper.

Printed in the United States of America
Bloomington, IN

Dedicated To Both Of My Fathers

In Honor of My Heavenly Father

From the womb... You have been and always will be

the 'Best Thing' that ever happened to me

I AM YOUR SERVANT

Thank You for giving me the privilege of serving

You in so many awesome ways!

In Memory of My Earthly Father

Adam Henry White, Sr.

You told me I could be anything I wanted to be

And what I wanted to be more than anything

was a consecrated vessel

In the hands of Almighty God

I AM YOUR DAUGHTER

Thank you for your love, *your* life, *and your* legacy

ACKNOWLEDGMENTS

Thanks Mom, **Mrs. Maybelle White**, for setting an example of diligence in everything you put your hands to. My husband, **Rev. Gregory Reed**, you have been my greatest teacher. Thanks for every valuable lesson. My best friend, **Beverly Gibson (Bevy G.)**, for your prayers, pushing, proofreading, and too many things to name…*Thank you!*

To my very own **Katherine Dunn**…in every endeavor and every test your encouragement was always the same. You told me it'll all work out…and it did! My daughter, **Harlena,** and my niece, **Miss O**, for listening to bits and pieces until it became a real book. You girls actually made me think I could write. **Bro. Herman Liggins**, for your support on every project. **Evang. Paula Tatum**, for fearlessly speaking into my life the things that are now coming to pass. **Hulah Gene Hurley**, thanks for showing your faith in me with a tangible investment in this project. **Doris Pugh,** for your patience and calming influence when I was down to the wire. **Evang. Pat Campbell-Williams**, for being the faithful keeper of my hair. Your styles always make me feel like holding my head high as I step into my destiny. To **Every Person** who facilitated my journey in any way…

From The Depths Of My Heart
Thank You

Table Of Contents

PART ONE
Of Things Seasonal

Table of Contents

PART TWO

Strategies Of Surrender

INTRODUCTION

Wherever you are on your Christian journey, you will find yourself in this book! If you've walked with God 30 days or 30 years, there will always be something from your heart, that God wants in His hands. Some call it surrender, and others say that God just wants you to give Him a 'yes'.

Surrender leads us to the very center of God's will, and ensures safe arrival at the destination of His choosing.

When our heart's desire is to follow the path God has chosen, it can never be a question of what may be required. It can only be, that we willingly lay at His feet, anything He asks. God never challenges us to give up something, without giving us the power to let it go!

As you read the pages of this book, my prayer is that you would zero in on your present location, and ask Him to take you to 'The Other Side Of Yes'.

PART ONE

Of Things Seasonal

THIS IS MY FATHER'S WORLD

This is my Father's world, And to my list'ning ears

All nature sings, and round me rings The music of the spheres.

This is my Father's world, I rest me in the thought

Of rocks and trees, of skies and seas - His hand the wonders wrought.

This is my Father's world, The birds their carols raise;

The morning light, the lilly white, Declare their Maker's praise.

This is my Father's world, He shines in all that's fair;

In the rustling grass I hear Him pass, He speaks to me everywhere

This is my Father's world, O let me ne'er forget

That though the wrong seems oft so strong, God is the Ruler yet.

This is my Father's world, The battle is not done;

Jesus, who died, shall be satisfied, And earth and heav'n be one.

Malthie D. Babcock 1901

FROM THE WOMB

Jer. 1:5 *"I knew you before I formed you in your mother's womb. Before you were born I set you apart and appointed you as my spokesman to the world."* (NLT)

The things you are about to read in this book are not fictional. In some shape, form, or fashion I've had to live every one of them. This document of deliverance has been in my spirit for nearly 10 years, but the call to write it has been with me from the womb. I was set apart to endure and survive the things that give this book the power to change your life. If you are serious about telling God to have His way, this is your passport.

With all humility, I accept His appointment to be a spokesperson to the world. It hasn't been easy to keep saying yes, but truly, it has been worth it! Even through my struggles, I have always found a way to praise God in the midst. Sometimes I praised Him because it was the *right* thing to do. Other times I did it because it was the *only* thing to do; but always because He was worthy of the praise!

This is not a step by step formula. It's a little nugget book, that speaks from the seasons of nature and the substance of life. May each nugget you find, yield a rich surrender to the perfect will of God.

YES, THERE IS A STRUGGLE!

Lord, I really do want You to have Your way, and I know it's the best thing for me, so why am I struggling? Help me God, I can't do this thing by myself! Every time I try to do what You ask, something keeps pulling me to go another way. Will I ever get it right?

If you've ever asked questions like these, you qualify for the journey to the other side of yes. Some people (even Christians), don't really care whether or not their lives bring God the kind of glory He deserves. Since you asked, I'm going to clue you in on what's happening.

To start this journey, I'll answer 2 key questions.

Why is there a struggle?

Where does the struggle come from?

Q. Why is there a struggle?

A. Rom. 7:21-23a makes it pretty plain. *"It seems to be a fact of life that when I want to do what is right, I inevitably do what is wrong. I love God's law with all my heart. But there is another law within me that is at war with my mind...."* (NLT)

The struggle exists because as human beings, our heart tells us one thing, but our mind is at war with the heart. Let's face it, the flesh has a mind of it's own!

Q. Where does the struggle come from?

A. Rom. 8:6-8 says, *"If your sinful nature controls your mind there is death. But if the Holy Spirit controls your mind, there is life and peace. For the sinful nature is always hostile to God. It never did obey God's laws and it never will. That's why those who are still under control to their sinful nature can never please God."* (NLT)

The struggle comes from fighting to surrender to the Holy Spirit, instead of our own will. Our fleshly reasonings try to convince us that God is asking more of us than we should be required to give.

Rom. 8:5 tells us how we can fix the problem, and that's what this book is all about. *"For they that are after the flesh do mind the things of the flesh; but they that are after the spirit, the things of the Spirit"* (KJV)

If you want to receive the things of the Spirit, then you must give attention to spiritual things more than you give to the things of your flesh. Simple things like taking time to pray when you feel the Lord moving on you. Read the scriptures not just out of duty, but listen for God to speak a life changing word. Discern the spiritual lessons in life's daily activities. All these things are small ways to strengthen the Spirit's presence, power and control in your life.

THE CONCEPTION OF A 'YES'

So where does 'yes' come from? Do we create it ourselves? I don't think so. Every good and perfect gift comes from God. The ability to surrender is a gift from God that enables us to effectively carry out His plans. The act of surrender is our part of the process. Planting the desire is a sovereign work of God. Surrender is our agreement to carry the seed.

The ability to surrender is a gift from God that enables us to effectively carry out His plans

---

Phil. 2:13 says, *"For God is working in you, giving you the* **desire** *to obey him and the* **power** *to do what pleases him."* (NLT) I also like the King James Version of this passage, which reads, *"For it is God that worketh in you both to* **will** *and to* **do** *of His good pleasure."*

Whatever God gives to us, He has the right to expect a return. We have things somewhat imbalanced in our 'name it and claim it,' *church* theology. Too much emphasis is placed on giving and expecting a return from God. What about the things God has freely given to us? Sowing and reaping is a Biblical principle, so God has just as much right to anticipate something from us. Everything we have, He gave us in the first place. The

Bible says in **I Chron.29:14b** *"...for all things come of Thee, and of Thine own have we given Thee."* (KJV)

I ran across a verse in a little 1/2 off card shop that really drove the point home. On the cover of a card by Hanoch McCarty was a lone pine tree in full bloom, with its branches casting a deep shadow on snow covered terrain. In the distance, smaller greenery sprouted on a white mountainside, laid against a rich azure sky. The photography alone was inspirational enough, but the words on the cover opened up a well of thought. Here's what it said...'YOU gave me **roots**, I give you b r a n c h e s'.

When it comes to saying 'yes', God gives us the root system of desire, and the power to nurture and grow whatever it takes to produce the branches of surrender. He gives us the **desire** to surrender, and the **power** to carry out the act. If God didn't plant the desire on the inside, we wouldn't even recognize that surrender is the thing we need to do.

THE BUDDING OF A 'YES'

The process of budding is when development begins. So how do you develop a surrender? Surrender is when you give up your power over something, and yield it to somebody else. The conception of a yes is God *planting* in us the 'will'. The budding of the yes is God *working* in us the 'do'.

**Surrender is when you give up
your power over something,
and yield it to somebody else**

One of the greatest struggles for human beings is to give up control. There are many reasons why we have second and third thoughts about allowing God to take over the *process* of growing a surrender inside of us.

I'm going to use pregnancy in this section, because it's the closest concept to something growing on the inside. Don't put this book down Brothers, just hang in here with me. You'll get my point.

Some women receive a seed into their womb, become pregnant, then choose not to give birth. Here are a few possible reasons for having abortions.

* Not wanting to experience <u>discomfort</u> during fetal growth
* Not wanting to <u>change the normal shape</u> of things

* Feeling inadequate to face the <u>responsibility</u> that comes <u>after the birth</u>

* Having given birth to <u>enough children</u>

DISCOMFORT

When God first approaches us with the invitation to carry a seed, it makes us *uneasy*. We say things like:

"God, do You know what You're asking?" (of course He does)

"You expect me to change horses in the middle of the stream?"

(who created the horse?)

"People will think I'm crazy if I just up and… (so what else is new?)

"God, This is not a good time!" (can you pick one that is?)

How do you think Mary felt when the angel Gabriel came to her right in the midst of her comfort zone, and announced that she had been picked to receive a seed no one else in the *world* would ever carry. She could have objected right off the bat, but instead Mary asked one simple question, *"How shall this be, seeing I know not a man?"* (**Luke 1:34b, KJV**) God doesn't mind us asking some details about what we're in for. The key is in becoming comfortable with it once He sheds light on what we can handle.

CHANGING THE NORMAL SHAPE

We get real uptight about stepping out of what we consider normal, or what we *feel* is stable. God's plan can be aborted by viewing change as an enemy instead of an instrument. Surrender is usually not some bright idea to leave things the same. Even if a situation doesn't change right away, we're challenged to change our endurance level by receiving more grace to keep going through the same old stuff.

God's plan can be aborted by viewing change as an enemy instead of an instrument

---

In the course of thirty plus years of ministry, I have been led to 9 different churches, helping build, strengthen, correct, instruct, etc. During the first few moves, I was excited about having fresh impact on each congregation. Then it got to the point where I just wanted a little sense of stability. Forget fresh impact, I was tired of being moved around...even by *God*. Little did I realize that each assignment was preparation for a scope of ministry I could not fathom at the time.

Anyway, God would wait until I fell in love with the people, and vice versa, to begin changing the atmosphere, which led to the next move. It took a while for me to get a grip. I was there to get a job done, not to become a permanent fixture. The weekly fellowship would create such a comfort zone for me, and it was always difficult to give that up. When I fully committed myself to God's strategy, I understood that true stability is found in Him alone.

✷ INADEQUACY TO HANDLE RESPONSIBILITY

Most of us know that the 'other side of yes' has to hold new challenges, and a different set of responsibilities. If you feel like you're not up to a task, it can be overwhelming. What I love about God, is that He has

9

already anticipated every hindrance we could be confronted with. Not only that, but He has an antidote for every one.

Phil. 1:6 says, *"And I am sure, that God, who began the good work within you, will continue His work until it is finally finished on that day when Christ Jesus comes back again."* (NLT) What that says to me is that God won't start a thing without providing all the equipment to handle *stuff* on the way to the finish line. That's why it's imperative for Him to plant the seed. He is the faithful Overseer of what He initiates.

In 1984, I wrote and produced a concert-drama called, 'Eternal Life'. I'm not a woman with any college degrees, so every project God ever gave me required <u>total</u> dependence on His expertise. Nothing can ever substitute for the School of The Holy Spirit. God does use things we have acquired, but He also uses the fact that we have *not* acquired some things. What we don't have simply heightens our sense of true dependency on a more than capable God! A few of you needed that little boost of confidence.

What we don't have, simply heightens our sense of true dependency on a more than capable God!

In spite of having to write music, teach choir parts, train actors, sew costumes, design flyers, teach the Word in rehearsals, secure performance locations, draw up contracts, and so on.....not once in 8 years of performances did God ever fail to give me what I needed to keep from going over the edge.

Here's a nugget. God actually provided more help than I was willing to use. That sounds kind of dumb doesn't it? Well, it was, but I learned a HUGE lesson. At that time in my life, I was a perfectionist. In my mind, I just wanted things to be done in the spirit of excellence, but it was much worse than that.

If programs weren't folded with a straight crease down the absolute center I would go through and refold them. If a paper cutter left a sliver, I redid the cut with scissors. Much time was wasted inspecting jobs others had done, to see if they met my standards. The Lord had a remedy, though. I will never, ever forget the precious sisterfriend that taught me how to let go. It was crunch time for one of the productions, and I needed help to finish sewing costumes. I taught Sharon Sharp some of the things she knew about sewing, but I felt her craftsmanship far exceeded mine. The girl was awesome! Naturally, that perfectionist thing led me straight to Sharon.

When she picked up the phone, I explained my plight. Sharon listened like any good friend would, and then gave me a point blank NO. I couldn't believe what I heard, so I restated my case. Her answer didn't change, but this time she told me why. My standards were too high, and she wasn't even going to *try* to meet them.

ATTENTION! God will never set you up to be overwhelmed. You can, however, overwhelm yourself. He supplies the help, but we must allow people to be who they are, and not who we want them to be. We'll never discover what folks have to offer if we force them to clone our methods.

I'm not going to say I didn't get weary, but never overwhelmed. Because God planted the seed of that vision, it came to pass in excellence every single time, and I didn't spend one day in an asylum.

ENOUGH CHILDREN ALREADY

If you read the back cover you already know I'm the mother of several grown children. Before I ever gave birth to my first child, I prayed and asked God for six healthy children. (*Some of you are probably wondering if I spent some days in the asylum before the 'Eternal Life' production.*) I could not imagine having another baby after God had fulfilled my request. I like the way my husband put it. It took God six days to create the heavens and the earth, and He rested on the seventh day. If six was good enough for God, it was good enough for me.

Another reason for aborting the seed, is because we have said 'yes' to so many things in the past. We're familiar with the process, and not quite ready to repeat it. Not now...not so soon. We become leery of the pain associated with allowing God to cultivate another seed. That's where I am right now in my own life.

I'm tired of giving in over and over, without seeing some tiny token of acceptance for my sacrifice. It's not that I'm looking for a payday from God, but it's encouraging to know He's pleased with what I am doing. When God spoke of Jesus saying, *"This is my beloved Son in whom I am well pleased,"* that kind of validation was all He needed to endure the fasting and temptation that followed in the wilderness.

Here's where seasoned veterans really have to be on guard. We can become weary in well doing, because it seems as though other Christians who could care less about surrender, are reaping all kinds of blessings. Giving God permission to have His way in us can never be based on how we *feel*. It must be rooted in the knowledge that God would never allow conception, without having a plan for the pregnancy, the pain, and the parenting.

Giving God permission to have His way in us, can never be based on how we feel

---

If we truly love God, it can't matter how many times He asks us to carry another seed. There is no such thing as a spiritual contraceptive when it comes to protecting our hearts from the plan of God. If we allow conception, we agree to a full term pregnancy.

There is no such thing as a spiritual contraceptive when it comes to protecting our hearts from the plan of God

---

THE BLOOMING OF A 'YES'

I've seen young women who didn't want anyone to know they were pregnant. As long as they tried to hide it, the baby's growth seemed to be suppressed. When they came to grips, and admitted the truth, *show*time was on.

Even though we've agreed not to abort, many of us hesitate to show for various reasons. We don't want to openly acknowledge that God is calling us to do a particular thing, and we're afraid to own up to the pregnancy.

When I think back to God's call to conduct a tent crusade in the city of Detroit, without backing from any of the major church leaders, I was scared to share the vision. First of all, I was a woman in ministry. (strike1!) I had no idea where the financial support *could* come from. (strike 2!) The only tent I had ever dealt with was a makeshift sheet thing in the backyard, using cardboard boxes for furniture. (strike 3!) To compound matters, when I prayed about the seating capacity, God's answer was 1,000 when I had never housed more than 3 kids under that makeshift tent.

I didn't want the vision to show, because I was afraid that as a woman in ministry, people would not have the same confidence in my leadership as God did.

When we understand that it is God Who justifies, we gain the courage to say 'yes' to any task, knowing that He not only provides for the situation, but also prepares the servant. **Romans 8:31,33** lets us know that if God is for us, no one else *can* be against us and succeed. No one can make legitimate accusations about your qualifications if God is the One Who chose you. In other words, you can't be charged with incompetence for a job God called you to do. If He trusts you with a task, it can't matter who else doesn't. He's the Supplier, everyone else is just a buyer.

You can't be charged with incompetence for a job God has called you to do

---

As I feel the anointing, my prayer for someone right now is that you would receive the courage and confidence God is trying to give you to make an acceptance speech and announce that He has called you to a task bigger than yourself…not because of who you are, but more so because of who you are not, He is even now justifying and qualifying you for every aspect of this assignment in Jesus' name!

Again, I was afraid to show because I wasn't able to see where the support *could* come from. I went through a list of all my acquaintances, and family members. I even considered ministry friends and their friends, etc. For the life of me, I couldn't see how a tent, 1,000 chairs, dumpsters, port-a-johns, advertising, electricity, and so on could be financed with the resource pool I was looking at. I knew if I shared the vision, someone was bound to ask me where the money was coming from.

Faith talk had gotten me through smaller ventures, but this was the biggest challenge I had ever been asked to carry out. I didn't mind speaking what I believed God would do, but what if He didn't come through *exactly* like I said. The thought of failure or embarrassment was really keeping me from fully showing.

✱ Well, let me tell you something. God didn't do everything the way I thought He would, but in the end He did His thing! Not every one of those 1,000 seats was filled, but God sent a husband and wife team all the way from Australia just for the tent crusade, to let me know His purpose of having international representation was being fulfilled. He sent a magazine publisher form Atlanta, GA., that I never met, to speak a word into my life on the last night of the meeting. It was a word 'in season', about my future and my destiny. It was a word about how no man could take credit for the move of God that had taken place, or claim ownership of the giftings in my life. That word validated the reason for every negative thing that had happened to me during the actual crusade.

✱ There was a good mixture of blacks and whites under the tent, to symbolize God's desire for racial harmony in the body of Christ. Catholics and Protestants hugged and embraced one another during a season of reconciliation.

Let me give some honor right here. Had it not been for Fr. Mark Brauer, the Catholic priest who said 'yes' to meeting with us to hear the vision, there may not have been a tent raised on Catholic property, for a Spirit-filled, Holy Ghost, Citywide Crusade. God showed me that He opens doors no man can shut. I could not have paid for the kind, accommodating spirit of Fr. Mark, and the people of St. Gemma Parish! Pray for him that he would continue walking in the plan of God as an 'Agent of Change'.

Finances came, and finances went, and when they ceased, God's favor took over! A week after the last tent stake was removed, every bill was marked PAID IN FULL, and God had kept His promises.

Never be afraid to share what you see, for fear that you won't get to see what you share. A seed will never blossom as it should, if you don't acknowledge your pregnancy.

Never be afraid to share what you see for fear that you won't get to see what you share

---

My final reason for not wanting to show, was that I knew I *didn't* know. I've been a trailblazer most of my life, but this was one groundbreaking ceremony I was not eager to attend. I *did* know that there was a lot of work involved, and most of it would have to be done in the 'discovery zone'.

Nugget time…Discovery isn't all bad. The flip side of not knowing, is having to diligently seek God for constant guidance. I found more information than I needed on some things, because seeking was so intense. My co-laborer in the gospel, Evangelist Gloria Garner, put it this way, "If you see it, it ain't faith!"

What I couldn't see, I *had* to believe, and believe me, it took quantum leaps of faith. Once again, I knew if I made the announcement that I was carrying the seed of a tent crusade, somebody was bound to ask me what the game plan was. I had to get alright with being asked questions

I knew I couldn't answer, and confessing that I would have to look to God for every move.

When God leads us by His Spirit, it's OK not to know every detail when the mission begins. The key is to stay tuned to the directions given along the way. An assignment given by the Spirit doesn't bring ultimate glory to God if we try to carry it out in the flesh.

An assignment given by the Spirit doesn't bring ultimate glory to God if we try to carry it out in the flesh

---

Once you agree to carry the seed of any God-given task, and rid yourself of all excuses to abort it, the process begins to blossom. God now has permission to set His plan in full motion.

TURNING UP THE HEAT

Have you ever been in a situation where so many things were falling apart at the same time, that you asked God, "Is it me, or is it them?" One of the positive intentions of tribulation is to make you examine yourself.

When I feel like everything is closing in and things are getting hot, I start asking God to show me what I need to give up. What do I need to throw overboard? Is there some area where I haven't sold out? As much as we want to blame others, our baggage is usually the first stuff that needs to be tossed.

Don't think every time the heat is turned up, there's some master plot to make your life miserable. **I Pet. 4:12** says, *"Beloved think it not strange concerning the fiery trial which is to try you, as though some strange thing happened unto you."*(KJV) I have learned to value the fire in trials as an invitation to burn the unnecessary upon the altar of sacrifice.

I have learned to value the fire in trials as an invitation to burn the unnecessary upon the altar of sacrifice

---

NO MORE COVER-UPS

Summer is a time when warmer climates bring out things some of us would rather not see. People tend to dress with less. The less they have covered up, the more attractive some folks seem to feel. Then again, there's something about heat that makes us want to peel off layers. Are you starting to get the picture?

Part of the strategy of surrender involves being willing to get rid of cover-ups. Brokenness is what makes us attractive to God. **Ps. 34:18**... *"The Lord is nigh unto them that are of a* broken *heart, and saveth such as be of a contrite spirit."* (KJV) **Ps. 51:17** says, *"The sacrifice acceptable to God is a broken spirit; A broken and contrite heart, O God, Thou wilt not despise."* (RSV) That's the kind of look that causes Him to draw near to us.

When God is trying to straighten stuff out, our so-called outer beauty doesn't mean a thing. **Ps. 39:11**... *"When with rebukes you correct man for iniquity, You make his beauty melt away like a moth..."* (NKJV) Even our self-righteousness is filth to Him.

I've been told people can look in my eyes and tell what my emotional condition is, because I'm basically transparent. What you see, with me, is really what you get. But I don't just want to be that way with people. I want God to know that *I* know there's no need to try and cover up the stuff He already knows about me. How can you surrender something you're trying to hide?

TRANSITION

One of the most beautiful and fascinating times of the year is when leaves begin to change colors. It's interesting how that works. Plants use light from the sun to turn carbon dioxide and water into glucose, which we know better as photosynthesis. A chemical called chlorophyll is what actually makes it happen and gives leaves their green color.

As days get shorter the trees know it's time to prepare for winter, so they start shutting down their food-making process, and live off of what they stored during summer. That's when the green starts to disappear, and we begin to see orange and yellow colors. The reds are made when glucose gets trapped in the leaves after photosynthesis stops. The shades of brown come from waste left in the leaves. That's a nice little science lesson.

My, what we can learn from a tree. The tree prepares for the time food production ceases, by making good use of the sunlight in the right season. God deals with us in a similar manner. He doesn't usually come with a point blank demand for surrender. He prepares us with *mini-surrenders* to bring us to the point where we're ready to give up.

I clearly remember the amount of preparation it took for me to say yes to the homegoing of my Dad. It actually started several years prior to his transition. My Dad was a dialysis patient, and one day they discovered that he was bleeding rectally during his run on the machine. He was rushed

21

to the hospital across from the unit, but they couldn't find the source of the blood right away.

Let me give you a little background about this next scene. I'm the one in my family that's looked up to as this tower of strength who helps pray the rest of the clan through. Very rarely do I let my emotions go on the wild, and lose total control of myself. Not to mention that at my brother's girlfriend's funeral, I cried harder and louder than anybody. A family friend came up afterwards, and told me he started to escort me out just to help keep the peace. So, due to past history, I try to keep some semblance of composure in tough times.

I had a hard time even *thinking* about my Daddy leaving, and God knew it was going take a few dry runs to help a sista' out. So, when I heard my Dad was in the hospital, I just knew his time was up, even though he was very conscious, talking, not in any pain, etc. I called my youngest brother to let him know, and I just lost it! He probably thought I should have been hospitalized along with my Dad. They soon found the problem, and he was released in about 3 days. That was preparation.

In the six years or so that followed, Daddy would pass out from time to time after coming off the machine; but he would always tell me how beautiful it was, and how he really didn't want to come back to earth. That was part of my preparation too.

About a year before the final departure, I was sitting in my car waiting to take a senior citizen to the doctor. All of a sudden the thought of missing my Dad crossed my mind and guess what I did? The cry I had this time was different, though. I could *see* life without him, and I knew I would have to surrender to that reality some day.

Through each experience I was made a little stronger. Like the leaves, I gleaned from the *SONlight* to collect what I could in the proper season. I knew when transition came, I would need to draw from every one of those 'dry runs' to survive the change. I used what God had allowed, as building blocks to climb the mount of surrender.

**I used what God had allowed,
as building blocks to climb
the mount of surrender**

When the appointed season finally came, it was totally different than I ever dreamed it could be. My Dad had fallen out of a chair on Saturday, after having a full day at my cousin's housewarming. Sunday morning he was on my mind real strong, so I called and asked if he would let me take him to urgent care just to get checked out. Any other time he would have given me a little hassle, but this time he was willing to go.

At urgent care they discovered a hard spot on his foot, and said because he was diabetic, I had to take him to the main hospital for further examination. As usual, he joked in the ER about a cat having nine lives. After a few quick x-rays, a decision was made that my Dad needed to have part of his foot amputated, and if it didn't heal, they would have to cut him again, possibly up to the knee.

Even after coming out of surgery, Dad was so jovial, I had no inkling the leaf was about to change colors, and gently fall from the tree. Three days into his recovery, I asked him if the Lord had said anything. The answer was yes. The message was that he had completed the things God gave him to do, and now it was time to go.

I accepted what he said, even though things didn't look that way at the time. Now I knew that all the tears of yesterday had prepared me to go to the other side of yes. Not only was my Dad about to cross over, but God had brought me to the place where I could let him go without a struggle. What peace there is in yielding to the *Master* plan.

The culmination of my surrender came on the 10th day, when Daddy was in a coma, and my sister had just returned from Ohio to bid him goodbye. I leaned over and did something only the grace of God could have enabled me to do. Without a tear, I whispered into the ear of the man who planted the seed for my very existence, and courageously said, "Daddy, you can go now."

Never take for granted the previews God gives us along the pathway to surrender. Whether good or bad, they serve as ushers into the arena of upcoming events. Like the leaves, store each one to use when the time to say yes finally arrives.

'YES' MUST PASS THE TEST

Have you ever wondered if a tree feels anything when it begins to shed leaves? What if trees share bragging rights about who has the most beautiful colors, or whose leaves start changing first. *Sh-h-h-h...Listen*

HICKORY: You know this bronze really looks good on me.

BIRCH: Humph...my golden yellow beams like sunshine blowing in the wind.

MAPLE: But I got my color first, this orangish-red is what makes the route scenic.

Listen again, because the conversation changes when the wind begins to blow.

HICKORY: Hel-l-p! I'm being stripped. Oh no-o-o...all my branches are about to show!

BIRCH: No, no, please don't...just one leaf...please leave me just, just one...

MAPLE: Wait...wait...wait a minute...Oh my God...you're *killing* me!...

Like the leaves, we can feel ever so good about ourselves for the fact that we have started to change. Don't get too excited yet, because that change must undergo testing to see if it is legit. This section is for those who have already said yes, but find themselves still being stripped by strong, gusting winds.

In one particular test, I said yes to God in every way possible. I went to the church altar and told Him yes. In my private prayer time, I cried out surrender through a river of tears. Intercessors helped me pray through to give God a yes, *and still* the winds kept on blowing. That's when I discovered my 'yes' was being tested.

Surrender must be tried. Did you really mean it when you told God yes? If things start happening, and it's more than you bargained for, will you try to take it back?

The surrender of our Lord was tested in the garden of Gethsemane. In **Mark 14:34-36,** read this very graphic description of what Jesus felt and how He responded. "*He told them, my soul is crushed with grief to the point of death. Stay here and watch with me.*" *He went a little further and fell face down on the ground. He prayed that, if it were possible, the awful hour awaiting Him might pass Him by.* "*Abba, Father,*" *He said,* "*everything is possible for you. Please take this cup of suffering away from me. Yet I want your will, not mine.*" (NLT)

Jesus knew He had the power to ask His Father for the rescue squad and Calvary would have been a no-show. After the mob came to arrest Him in the garden, one of the disciples tried to save Jesus from destiny by cutting off the servant's ear. Jesus told him to put his sword away; because if escape was what He was looking for He could just call His Daddy for twelve legions of angels from the command post of glory. I love this next part. He went on to say in **Matt. 56:54,** "*But if I did, how would the scriptures be fulfilled that describe what must happen now?*" (NLT)

'Yes' has to pass the test in order to know it will work when the time comes to implement the fullness of God's strategy. My Lord's first surrender was in allowing Himself to be wrapped in human flesh and dwell among men. Everything else He endured on this earth, tested that surrender and proved that it was real. Calvary wasn't easy, but it worked because He passed all the tests in between.

In the name of Jesus, receive the grace you need to pass whatever test(s) are causing winds to keep blowing in your life. May God reveal your destiny, and place it before you as a reason to keep yielding to His plan. Amen

HOW

Let's go back to the leaves for a moment. Have you ever watched a gust of wind pick up a whole batch of leaves, and just scatter them everywhere? Now picture this. Suppose each leaf tried to tell the wind which direction they wanted to be blown, and exactly where they wanted to land. Major Chaos!!

How about being trapped in your own house, because a group of Oak leaves got together and piled themselves 5 feet high in front of the doorway. Okay, okay…so I have a vivid imagination, but I bet you got the point.

On one of my journeys to the city of 'Yesville', I made a rather startling discovery. I was allowing my yes to be tested, when I realized I had only given God half of what He was after. I agreed to *what* God wanted, but I had not surrendered to *how* He wanted to do it. If we don't yield to God's method, we set ourselves up for a chaotic journey.

The *act* of surrender is not necessarily the same as saying yes to the *method*. Suppose you tell God yes to an assignment to help bring about racial harmony. What if the method includes marrying someone of another race as part of the package? There's a good chance that some of us would abandon the mission because of the method.

**The act of surrender is not
necessarily the same as
saying yes to the method**

HOW. Such a small word with such a powerful meaning. From Webster's New World College Dictionary we get this: **How** 1. in what manner or way; by what means 2. in what state or condition 3. for what reason or purpose. When you say, "Have Your Way, Lord", you are telling Him that in whatever manner, by whatever means, and in whatever condition you might find yourself, He still retains the right to be Sovereign.

Mary was mentioned in an earlier chapter, and I'm going to expand on that. In **Luke 1:31-33,** Gabriel told her *what* was going to happen. Although she was just a young woman, she had the courage to ask the *how* question up front. That's probably when Mary became the Blessed Mother, because she was blessed to get an answer that quickly. God doesn't always reveal the *how* right away. Sometimes it's just show and tell.

In **vs. 35-37,** she gets the scoop on the unconventional way the *what* is going to happen. That would have been a good time to turn down the assignment, but between Gabriel's appearance and his departure, two statements were made that gave Mary all the assurance she would ever need. We can take these same two proclamations and be OK with any manner God chooses to carry out His program. The angel came to Mary announcing, **"The Lord is with you,"** and closed by declaring, **"For with God nothing will be impossible."** That's all we really need to know. We have His presence *(God is with us),* and His power *(nothing is impossible),* to accomplish everything in the Divine Design.

Mary didn't fight God's method or the condition she knew she would be in because of it. Her concession speech was, "I am the handmaiden of the Lord, be it done unto me according to Your word." After Mary accepted the *what* and the *how*, everything she needed was revealed step by step from conception to delivery. God gave her a praise song; a cousin who could relate to the oddity of her situation; and Joseph, who listened to God's messenger and took her as his wife in spite of premarital impregnation by the Holy Ghost! Then He used an unlikely itinerary to lead her to the appointed stable. Know this, that whenever God gives a promise, He has already selected the path to pursue, and it will lead to the place of fulfillment.

THE WINTER OF OUR CONTENTMENT

Winter is the season that gives us a snuggly, cozy, cuddly feeling of true comfort. When snow blankets the earth, and icicles glisten on tree limbs, there's nothing like being in front of a live fireplace. Wood is crackling, and the sight of glowing embers gives you the warm fuzzies all over. Ah-h-h…yes.

If you can relate to any of those things, you can appreciate the contentment that comes from surrender. The rest and comfort of knowing you have given God the most important thing He could ask, is one of the first benefits of going to the other side of yes.

You might wonder how I can say that surrender is the most important thing God could ask. Think about it. When God draws a sinner to repentance, what do they need to do…*surrender!* When we are being dealt with about forsaking some sinful habit as believers, what is God really asking us to do…*surrender!* If He beckons us to operate in a gift or calling, and we feel inadequate, what do we know God is requiring of us…*surrender!* It's always about telling the Lord He can do it His way, in His time, and for His pleasure.

It's always about telling the Lord He can do it His way, in His time, and for His pleasure

Every single time we give God what He is calling for, there is a huge sigh of relief. Whatever we wrestled with before giving in, the struggle ceases…it's over. We can take a deep breath and exhale because we know we have brought a smile to the Father's face. That's real contentment.

Contentment is being OK with any circumstance God has ordered for your life. The apostle Paul said it best in **Phil. 4:6,** *"I know both how to be abased, and I know how to abound: everywhere and in all things, I am instructed both to be full and to be hungry, both to abound and to suffer need."* (KJV)

There was something God had promised me, and I wanted it like, yesterday. He let me know that I wasn't going to get it until *many* tomorrows. I pitched a couple of fits to get my will out of the way. Then He kindly brought me to the place of freedom and acceptance. God spoke to my heart that day and let me know that I was *just where He wanted me to be.* It was so real, and it felt so good to be assured that it was OK to wait for the due season. I had contentment. This is a poem I wrote about the experience.

SO WHERE YOU WANT ME TO BE

I am so where You want me to be
Though the future may be farther than I can see
Right now I'm so content, knowing that I've been sent
Exactly to the place You planned for me.

I see just what I need to see right now

And it's because I have chosen, Lord, to bow

At Your feet in humble praise, knowing that You guide my days

And whatever else I need You'll show me how.

Everything I need to use is in my hand

And it will be multiplied at Your command

As You send me forth I'll go, because this one thing I know

If I use what You gave me, I can stand.

HAPPY BIRTHDAY, JESUS...ALL YEAR LONG

The greatest holiday of the whole year rolls around every winter on December 25th. One of the reasons people give gifts at Christmas is to show how much they care. We ask the big question way ahead of time..."What do you want for Christmas?' No matter the answer, we either prepare to make sacrifices or make bills. Somehow I believe the folks we value the *most*, receive the *best* we can buy. You see where I'm headed, don't you?

I value Jesus more than anyone and anything, and I just believe He deserves the best I can give. Surrender is not only the best gift, but it's the gift that keeps on giving all year long. God never grows weary of receiving it, and each time we give it, it's new all over again.

In December of 2002 God asked me to give HIM an early Christmas present. It kinda' shocked me, because I thought I had already given Him this particular gift. Here's what He asked..."Give me you heart, undivided...let Me work in it what I will...give Me your heart...yes, I have made promises to you, and all of My promises are true...but give Me your heart...surrender every *thought*, every *desire*, every *design*...let Me order every step...you WILL see all of My good pleasure come to pass in your life...nothing will stop your destiny...only give Me your heart..."

Now that's a full bodied description of surrender! Every thought, every desire, every design. My WHOLE heart!! I was on my way, going full speed ahead, loving God with all my heart, and ready to step into my promises. *But what happened was*, I had my own thoughts about how God should <u>design</u> my <u>desires</u>. He asked me to release those things, so the journey would be according to His way and not my own.

The plea broke me down. God gave me my heart, so how could I tell Him He couldn't recapture it just for the asking? I didn't take time to think about my answer, it just began to flow. "Lord, I realize that I am not my own, for truly I have been bought with the greatest price any father could pay...the blood of Your only begotten Son...the life of Your firstborn...I have no rights except You give them to me. Take my heart and do with it what you will and what you must!"

Have you given your whole heart? Will you surrender to God, those things you feel are rightfully yours? **Now** is the appointed season to give Jesus the gift that celebrates the Life He gave for us, and the heart He gave to His Father.

PART TWO

Strategies Of Surrender

I SURRENDER ALL

All to Jesus I surrender, All to Him I freely give;
I will ever love and trust Him, In His presence daily live.
All to Jesus I surrender, Humbly at His feet I bow,
Worldly pleasures all forsaken, Take me, Jesus, take me now.
All to Jesus I surrender, Make me, Savior, wholly Thine;
May Thy Holy Spirit fill me, May I know Thy pow'r divine.
All to Jesus I surrender, Lord I give myself to Thee;
Fill me with Thy love and power, Let Thy blessing fall on me.

I surrender all,
I surrender all.
All to Thee, My blessed Savior,
I surrender all.

Judson W. VanDeVenter 1896

NO AGENDA...NO RESISTANCE

I'm quite a people watcher, and I've observed a powerful key to this 'whole heart' thing. For about a year, I watched the phenomenal spiritual growth of a young man by the name of Quintin Thomas. I met Quintin when my youngest son brought him to a prayer meeting at the house. My first thought was, what kind of unchurched 18 year old would willingly come to a prayer meeting just because he was invited?

It was a *real* different experience for him, but he was open. Whatever God was handing out that day, he wanted some of it. When I say different, I'm talking about the difference between a reserved, laid back, conservative setting, and a knockdown, drag out, Holy Ghost move of God.

As Quintin tells it, he was a little scared at first; but then he *felt* God, and it gave him a sense of safety. Things haven't been the same since. The intense hunger and realness of that experience created a passion in him to seek God at all costs.

Here's the key. In Quintin's encounter with God, he didn't have an agenda of his own. Since he had no set plan to present, God was able to write His own agenda on the blank slate of Quintin's heart. When we have no personal agenda, we tend to offer no resistance.

When we have no personal agenda, we tend to offer no resistance

An agenda is a program of things to be done. How many times have you set up your own system, without bothering to ask the Lord for any guidance, approval, or even input? Do you realize you're shortchanging yourself if you don't take advantage of **Prov. 3:5**? Acknowledging God before planning holds the promise of receiving His direction. It also allows Him to give you His agenda, before you have a chance to set up your own.

One of the things I share with young believers is to always make sure you get God's answer regarding your plans. When the going gets tough, you can always go back to Him and say, "OK, You told me to do this, so You're obligated to fix whatever ain't workin'."

Guess what? It works! Try it! He never lets go of the helm, if you give Him permission to steer.

I think the biggest problem God has with us is having too much pride to admit when we've missed it. The reason David acknowledged his wrong so freely in Psalm 51, was that He didn't want God to take His spirit away. I would rather confess my wrong and have God's presence, than to risk shipwreck trying to press past His counsel. Do I ever have a great example of that!

In the year 2000, a small nucleus of sisters labored together to host an awesome conference called 'Women Of Courage, Standing On The

Rock'. I was one of the primary decision makers, and of course one of the first to receive blame if something didn't appear to be going right.

We had intercessors that started praying nine months before the conference. God took every request, and ordered our steps right into the path of Divine favor. Once the presence of God showed up at the conference, it never left. All kind of wonderful testimonies were shared, and we could hardly wait for the next one.

Based upon these rave reviews of the 'move of God', we started planning **WOC 2001.** The place where we had the first conference was closing down for renovation, and another location had to be picked. A committee was formed to tour a facility in Battle Creek, MI. Everything looked perfect! We were given free sweatshirts, a complimentary lunch, the works!...but something didn't *feel* right.

I zoomed right on past that feeling. WOC 2000 had been so great, would God do anything less in 2001? The agenda was set. People were crying out for more, and WOC was going to meet the need! I put down $200 of my personal funds for the deposit, just to show God that I believed in His ability to 'do it again'. All of that being done, I still couldn't get away from the nagging thought that something wasn't right.

The intensity and the fervor that accompanied the first conference was lacking. I had struggled with other projects, but that was simply spiritual warfare. The enemy never wants anointed works to succeed. But this struggle was unfamiliar to me, and I knew I had to stop and seek God for an answer.

NUGGET TIME! If you are a leader, always be willing to examine yourself first. It would have been so easy for me to say, "What's wrong with these sisters? They were so fiery last time, and now they just don't seem to be able to move this thing?" It is so convenient to find someone else to help shoulder the blame.

In my seeking, God spoke four words that taught me never to be presumptuous with Him again. Are you ready for this? Here it is. ***YOU DIDN'T ASK ME***! How profound...how simple...how foolish not to consult Him every time. God is the only One Who knows where He's going to show up and when., If He sets the agenda, His presence is guaranteed.

I had to be a real Woman Of Courage, to share with the committee what God had spoken. Everybody's reaction was pretty much the same. What a simple, yet vital thing to overlook. For whatever reason, the conference did not take place. I was blessed to transfer the deposit to another group, but the lesson was invaluable and worth every bit of the shame. It always pays to 'phone first', even when we're calling heaven.

Think about it though. I could have resisted what the Lord was speaking. The agenda was already set, but my resistance would have been all about pride. It's not worth holding on to our plans at the expense of letting go of God's presence and approval.

No agenda...No Resistance!

RESISTANCE IS COSTLY

Whenever I make a purchase, I hunt for the best possible bargain. If you weigh the cost of resistance against the cost of surrender, it's clear to see which one is most cost effective. I've called on three brothers and one sister from the pages of scripture to testify about the price they paid for resistance or rebellion.

JONAH

Resistance to where God wanted him to go (**Jonah 1:3**)

Cost...A 3 day belly ride sponsored by Divine Fish Enterprises (**Jonah 1:17**)

MIRIAM

Rebellion against Moses' leadership and marriage (**Num. 12:1,2**)

Cost...Miriam became 'Snow White' (a leper), with 7 days exile instead of 7 dwarfs. (**Num. 12:14**)

ACHAN

Rebellion against God's covenant with Israel (**Josh. 7:11**)

Cost...A fiery exit with a heap of family memorial stones (**Josh. 7: 25,26**)

ELI, THE PRIEST

Resistance to proper discipline of his sons in the priesthood (**I Sam. 2:29**)

Cost…Both his sons were killed on the same day, and Eli did a slow motion, backwards flip into eternity. (**I Sam 4:17,18**)

That's enough to make the point. Let me conclude this section with something I said to my niece not long ago. We were talking about the things people go through, including myself, in order to maintain a heavy anointing upon their lives. Some Christians shun Godly sacrifices because the pricetag is too high. I have a totally different way of looking at it. If you think you pay a high price for an anointing, you pay twice as much for a hard head. Spare your head, by willing submission to God's agenda.

If you think you pay a high price for an anointing, you pay twice as much for a hard head

---

GOD HAS A STRATEGY

My very best friend is Beverly Ann Gibson, affectionately known as Bevy G. (*the names I use in this book are people destined to have great Kingdom impact...I'm just making a few early introductions*) She is by Divine appointment, an intercessor, preacher, prophetess and teacher of the Word.

I love the way the girl dissects words. The other day Bev got a hold of the word *strategy,* and turned it into a dynamite study session. I want to share a little about post-surrender strategy. Much of this book deals with things that lead up to the door. On the other side of yes is a strategy for working out the details of what you have surrendered to.

The chief thing to remember is that saying yes brings inner peace, but doesn't necessarily mean the journey will be free of challenges. Strategies are made up of the schemes used to achieve a purpose. Strategy is what carries us from surrender to successful completion.

Another thing to think about is this. Surrender doesn't mean a whole lot if we don't follow through with the strategy.

Surrender doesn't mean a whole lot if we don't follow through with the strategy

---

Whenever you think about saying yes and fail to commit your actions, remember the parable in **Matt. 21:28-31**.

"But what do you think about this? A man with two sons told the older boy, 'Son, go out and work in the vineyard today.' The son answered, 'No, I won't go,' but later he changed his mind and went anyway. Then the father told the other son, 'You go,' and he said, 'Yes, sir, I will.' But he didn't go. Which of the two was obeying his father? They replied, "The first, of course." Then Jesus explained his meaning: "I assure you, corrupt tax collectors and prostitutes will get into the Kingdom of God before you do." (NLT)

I don't know about you, but I wouldn't want to go through all it takes to surrender, and then miss out on God's best because I couldn't follow the strategy.

SAY 'YES' TO RECONCILIATION

Matt. 5:23,24 *"So if you are standing before the altar in the temple offering a sacrifice to God, and you suddenly remember that someone has something against you, leave your sacrifice there beside the altar. Go and be reconciled to that person"* (NLT)

One of the things that can keep us from total surrender is being unwilling to reconcile with those who have wronged us or feel we have wronged them. Scripture tells us that if we *remember* our brother has an ought against us, GO! The essence of **Matt. 5:23, 24** is not to try to offer something to God, if we *know* things are not right with someone else.

The passage speaks of leaving the altar to get it straight. An altar is simply a place where sacrifice is made. Surrender is the sacrifice of one's self. How can we truly give ourselves to God, if we knowingly allow an ought to remain without trying to do something about it?

How can we truly give ourselves to God, if we knowingly allow an ought to remain without trying to do something about it?

You're reading this book, so it proves you're not brain dead. Please don't try to act like you don't know when someone has a problem with you!

At the first inkling that a brother or sister has an issue with you, prayerfully search yourself. If you sense any possible offense on your part, GO! Ask if you did something that caused a problem. If the answer is yes, go ahead and give an apology or whatever may be needed. Even if they say no, (whether true or not), at least you've opened the door for God to move, and the ball is no longer in your court. This might sound elementary, but some Christians act like they don't know how to seek reconciliation.

Here's a nugget for any reconciliatory situation. When you go to a person, humble yourself. Christ was willing to take the blame even though He wasn't guilty. Try not to point the finger, but accept the weight of responsibility for getting things straight. It also causes the other person to look inwardly. That was, after all, the mindset of Calvary. Jesus carried the burden and punishment of something He didn't do. When you look at yourself in light of that, it makes you want to get right with God!

Attempts at reconciliation may not always work, but you must be willing to try (perhaps more than once). Seeking the face of God isn't worth much if you can't freely look into the face of your brother or sister, knowing every attempt has been made to settle an issue.

NEVER FAIL TO FORGIVE

Matt. 6:15 *"But if you refuse to forgive others, your Father will not forgive your sins."* (NLT)

An unwillingness to forgive can be one of the biggest roadblocks to reaching the other side of yes. In **Matthew 6:9-15**, we find the prayer example that Jesus gave when the disciples asked Him to teach them how to pray. Forgiving others their trespasses was the only concept from the prayer that Jesus took the time to reiterate. It had to be pretty important. He went on to say that if we chose not to forgive, we wouldn't be forgiven by God. Now that's some strong, scary stuff.

Remember that surrender means to give up yourself to another's power or control. In this case of course, we're talking about giving control to God. How can you freely give yourself to God when someone else is chained to you as a prisoner of your unforgiveness? There's no way you can give God total control, if you are exercising control over someone else's life, by your refusal to release them from wrongs they've done.

How can you freely give yourself to God when someone else is chained to you as a prisoner of your unforgiveness?

I love God for how He deals with us if we let him. He is so faithful to bring before us the people we have not forgiven. I remember going to a retreat center to scope out the territory for a women's conference. While I was alone, God took me to the book of Matthew, the 6th chapter. I had an unforgiveness issue, and He used that time to 'get with me'. What really killed me, was the version of the Bible I was reading at the time.

Matt. 6:15 *But if you do not forgive others their trespasses [their <u>reckless</u> and <u>willful</u> sins, leaving them, letting them go, and <u>giving up resentment</u>], neither will your Father forgive you your trespasses.* (Amplified Bible)

The underlined words are my own emphasis. It's easier to forgive people that hurt you big, and then they walk away. Reckless and willful, makes me think of someone hurting you time and time again, intentionally, and having no conscience behind it. Guess what? No matter how people have treated us or what they've done, forgiveness is not an option. It is a prerequisite for getting to the other side of yes.

SAY 'YES' TO BEING BROKEN

Ps. 34:18 *"The Lord is near to the brokenhearted and saves the crushed in spirit."*(NRSV)

For several years now, prophetic words have come into my life regarding stepping out into international ministry. So many times it looked like I was right on the edge of a breakthrough, but it didn't happen. I finally got the answer when I least expected it. There is a difference between breaking and being broken. To *break* according to Webster's New World College Dictionary, is to diminish or discontinue abruptly; to render useless and inoperable; to snatch off or detach. Whereas, to be *broken* is to be subdued, trained and tamed.

The Lord let me know that I had to endure many breakings, before I was actually broken. What He had allowed in the breaking processes was training me and taming me, so my will and my flesh could be subdued under His mighty hand. Now that I understand, I no longer have the desire to dictate or even suggest to God, what I do or don't *feel* like going through. I realize that it's foolish to try and tell Him I've been in the storm too long. He orchestrated the storm, and I trust Him enough to know that He'll speak to the wind and the waves at the right time, and say, "Peace Be Still."

I've been trained to know that the quicker I surrender, the sooner I get to walk into my next season. I've been tamed. I no longer growl at the

50

Trainer. When I feel the pain of life's *whip*ping circumstances, I know it's time to lay down, be still, and know He is God.

It's even alright to cry, but you can't work God with your tears. I've cried, kicked, stomped and screamed, and God's only response was, "Are you finished yet?" Then, He gave me more grace, so I could keep going through until it was time to come out.

What happened to the fish and loaves in **Luke** chapter **9** is what must take place in us if we want to be given to the *multitudes*. **Vs. 16** says," "Then He took the five loaves and the two fish, and looking up to heaven, He blessed and broke *them*, and gave *them* to the disciples to set before the multitude." (NKJV)

If you want God to use you to the fullest, stop trying to avoid painful processes. They lead to precious promises. Neither should you fear, because God is going to do the same thing He did in vs.16, before the breaking. He blessed! Just trust Him, for in the blessing will be everything you need to survive.

**If you want God to use you to the fullest,
stop trying to avoid painful processes**

On the other side of yes is the privilege of letting God use your life as sustenance for the multitudes. You may not stand before crowds of thousands; but one by one, every single person you come in contact with will know they can draw deeply from the Christ in you because you've been blessed and broken.

Right now in the name of Jesus, my prayer for you is that the spirit of fear, and the dread of feeling pain would be broken off your life. May you be anointed with the courage to step out on the blessing and let God have His way.

BE WILLING TO WAIT

Isa. 40:31 *"But those who wait on the Lord will find new strength.*
They will fly high on wings like eagles. They will run and not grow weary.
They will walk and not faint." (NLT)

I love the definition for wait in the Webster's New World College Dictionary. It means to stay in a place or remain in readiness or in anticipation until something expected happens.

Life seems to overflow with opportunities for waiting. We wait in all sorts of lines, at doctor's offices, for debts to be repaid, curfew breaking teenagers, broken bones to mend, babies to be born, and the list goes on. In many cases, we wait whether we choose to or not.

When it comes to God, how *willing* we are to wait makes all the difference. We may find ourselves having to remain in a place, but not necessarily with anticipation. Here goes Webster's again. To be willing is to be consenting; acting readily and cheerfully. In order to appreciate cheerful waiting, we need to understand the benefits of waiting on God.

Isa. 40:31 tells us the primary benefit of waiting is the renewal of strength. In verses **29** and **30** we read about souls in various stages of weariness. The faint, those who have no might, youths who get weary and young men that fall. They all have to make their way to the **A** part of verse **31**. I see them staggering, reeling, and falling prostrate at the throne of the

Almighty, doing whatever it takes to wait in His presence, because they know the strength to survive is the reward just for being there.

The strength to wait can only come from spending adequate time in the presence of God

---

Surrender usually requires a span of time between the thing you've said yes to, and the outworking of the plan that leads to a manifestation. You have to be able to walk it out and not grow weary. The only way to do that is to be willing to wait. The strength to wait can only come from spending adequate time in the presence of God.

REMOVE THE RESTRICTIONS

Rom. 11:33 *"Oh, what a wonderful God we have!*
How great are His riches and wisdom
and knowledge! How impossible it is for us
to understand His decisions and His methods." (NLT)

Surrender is unconditional! You can't tell God you give up, and follow it with, *"but only if..."* Access is not available to the other side of yes, if you try to get through the door with self-imposed restrictions. Picture this. The Lord opens a door for you to speak out of town, and you tell Him OK, *but only if* you can take your family. So here you go with one child hanging from around your waist, another one holding onto your ankle, being dragged sideways, and your spouse perched on top of your head. When you get to the doorjamb, everybody won't fit, so what are you going to do?

If we try to place our restrictions on God's methods, somebody's going to lose, and it's not going to be God. I'm sure He can find someone else who's willing to do things His way.

Another thing we do in the area of restrictions is to give God deadlines. Now there's a difference when He gives us a time frame. We can count on that to come to pass exactly the way He said. The word to Sarah in **Gen.18:10** was that she would have a child about one year from the time the promise was made. Of course in **Gen. 21:2**, we see God did it like He said it.

Speaking from a multitude of personal experience, you can encounter a lot of disappointment trying to tell God when. I want to highlight David's journey in **Ps. 31**, starting with something he says in **vs. 2**, and following his thought process through **vs. 15**. At the start (**vs. 2**), David cries out for God to deliver him *speedily*. Then he goes on to give God some kudos. You're a rock of refuge…a fortress of defense…do it for Your namesake, O God.

Vs. 4…pull me out of the net…You are my strength.

Vs. 5…I commit my spirit to you…You're a God of truth.

Vs. 6…I trust You Lord.

Vs. 7…I rejoice in Your mercy…You know my soul in adversities.

Vs. 8…You have set my feet in a wide place.

He starts feeling the depths of his condition starting with **vs. 9.**

Vs. 9…I'm in trouble…I'm wasting away, body and soul.

Vs. 10…My strength fails…I am consumed with grief.

Vs. 11…I'm a reproach to enemies and friends…Folks are running from me.

Vs. 12…I'm like a dead man…Out of sight, out of mind…I'm broken.

Vs. 13…People are talking about me…They want to kill me.

In **vs. 14** *and* **15,** *David heads back to* **vs. 6,** *but things are a little differen*

Vs. 14…I trust You, Lord…You are my God

Vs. 15…*My times are in Thy hands.*

David goes from asking God to deliver him speedily to acknowledging that no matter how difficult the case, and how quickly he wants out...his times for deliverance are in God's hands.

I've been heartbroken and put to shame by the number of times I gave God parameters He simply refused to operate within. Now I know that it was for my own good. Surrender must always be on God's terms, if we want to make it to the other side.

SAY 'YES' TO FREEDOM

John 8:36 *"If the Son therefore shall make you free,
you shall be free indeed."* (KJV)

Congratulations! You made it! True freedom is yours if you hold fast to what you received from this book. You are released from the prison of your own will, and God can do a work, because your surrender has given Him permission to proceed.

Some of you will encounter freedom from physical ailments, because you chose to go to the other side of forgiveness. Many of your physical infirmities were caused by spiritual bondage and bitterness. You can breathe better now, and allow God to release His love through you to the one you once held captive. Walk in peace, beloved, determined never to take another hostage.

Others had already forgiven, but didn't want to take the extra step to *seek* reconciliation. You had adopted the adage about 'loving from a distance', If real love could be done from a distance, then perhaps our Saviour would never have left the glories of heaven. He took on human flesh just to die on Calvary's cross, proving the depths of God's love. He could have saved Himself the trip, and just loved us from a distance, but salvation would not be ours today. On the other side of yes you may just discover that some forgiven person is waiting for you to invite them back to the arms of your acceptance. You're free now to go. Seek out the lame, and restore them to wholeness.

You are free now, to let God set the boundaries and the terms for surrender. It's no longer your responsibility for struggling to figure out the how, when and where of every assignment. Your times are in His hands, and when the time is right, God will fill you in on everything you need to know to get the job done His way. Because you crossed over to the other side by removing selfish restrictions, you'll hear God much clearer when He speaks.

I join with you in praising God for every surrender that came from the depths of your heart, allowing you to move freely into your destiny! Walk on through the door now. Turn the knob to victory and get to steppin' to **The Other Side Of....**

Yes!

THE MOST IMPORTANT SURRENDER

Perhaps you picked up this book in search of something and you really didn't know what it was. You can say yes to God in any area mentioned in this book, but unless you say yes to His gift of salvation, nothing else matters. Just in case you don't know, it is my privilege to tell you how.

God loves you.

"For God so loved the world, that He gave His only begotten Son, that whoever believes in Him should not perish, but have eternal life" (John 3:16).

Man is separated from God by sin.

"For all have sinned and fall short of the glory of God" (Romans 3:23). "For the wages of sin is death" (Romans 6:23).

The death of Jesus Christ in our place is God's only provision for man's sin.

"He (Jesus Christ) was delivered over to death for our sins and was raised to life for our justification" (Romans 4:25).

We must personally receive Jesus Christ as our Savior and Lord.

"But as many as received Him, to them He gave the right to become children of God, even to those who believe in His name" (John 1:12).

"For by grace you have been saved through faith; and that not of yourselves, it is the gift of God; not as a result of works, that no one should boast" (Ephesians 2:8, 9).